Coffee Drinks

Coffee Drinks

AN ILLUSTRATED INFOGRAPHIC GUIDE
TO WHAT'S IN YOUR CUP

Merlin Jobst

DOG 'n' BONE

Published in 2017 by Dog 'n' Bone Books
An imprint of Ryland Peters & Small Ltd
20–21 Jockey's Fields   341 E 116th St
London WC1R 4BW   New York, NY 10029

www.rylandpeters.com

10 9 8 7 6 5 4 3 2 1

A CIP catalog record for this book is available from
the Library of Congress and the British Library.

ISBN: 978 1 911026 23 5

Printed in China

Illustrator: Blair Frame
Editor: Nathan Joyce
Cover designer: Emily Breen

Contents

Introduction 6
A Bit on Beans 8

The Coffee Drinks

Introduction

Coffee can be as simple or complex as we want it to be. Historically, it's more than just a beverage; it's had an enormous stake in the development of civilizations and, as a commodity, it stands today as the second most traded in the world. It's also a highly evolved craft, with an almost endless number of forms. But at the same time, it's just coffee; the drink that keeps millions of us moving, and pausing, and connecting with one another. It's delicious, comforting, and adored, as well as being a whole world of history, expertise, and culture in itself.

Although knowing everything about coffee isn't essential, choosing to learn more can have an impact on how we enjoy it—from knowing whether we prefer brewed black coffee or Americano (and why), to understanding the subtle but crucial difference between a cappuccino and a flat white. We can notice when one coffee tastes more bittersweet, like (dark) chocolate, or is lighter in color when brewed than others. Or we can go deeper and connect its history—be it the myriad origin stories in the Middle East, or its role as the drink over which revolutionary movements blossomed in Europe centuries later—with the cup in front of us.

Then again, all we might want to bring to that are our own experiences; the sensory memories we have wrapped up in the inimitable bitterness of the coffee bean. But even these have cultural connotations. Whether our first memories of that flavor and aroma are familial (as is often the case in countries such as Italy, where coffee-drinking is encouraged as part of breakfast from an early age), or something associated with leaving home, or a first job, the way the world around us consumes coffee will have played a role in how we consume it.

But arguably the most important thing about coffee is that it can be enjoyed by anybody. That's why this book covers most of coffee's various forms, along with nuggets of history and trivia, without getting too bogged down by really geeky stuff. There's plenty of that out there, and the best bit is that going deeper—and if there's one thing to take away from this book, it's that there is always more to explore—can only improve your experience of coffee.

A Note

The coffee world is fraught with (mostly respectful) disagreements over almost every element of almost every coffee drink—from which is the best flavor profile for espresso to whether milk should wind up anywhere near the final product. While there is an admittedly broad consensus on ratios and measurements for most drinks, however, those provided in this book are to be treated as a guide. As they say in the trade, there's no single way to pull a shot.

A Bit on Beans

There's almost as much to know about coffee beans as there is about the many guises of the drink itself, ranging from the essentials (such as why roast color matters) and more intermediate (does it really make any difference to the end product where the beans were grown?), to the downright nerdy (what will the mouthfeel be like?). Luckily, beans are an extremely rewarding area of coffee to get into, because it fundamentally comes down to flavor; nothing shapes your drink more than what's been ground to make it.

Beans begin life as a berry (or "cherry") on the *Coffea* plant, of which there are two key varieties: *Arabica* and *Robusta*. The former is far more complex in its characteristics and is therefore more desirable, but also more difficult and expensive to grow. This means that Robusta, which incidentally has a naturally higher caffeine content than Arabica, is very commonly used by all corners of the mainstream coffee industry for a large percentage of their bean blends. *Coffea* cherries are ideally harvested when red and ripe, then dried and carefully roasted. The method of farming has a big impact on this process, because realistically only the human eye can be relied upon to tell which berries are ready to be harvested—or indeed, which bits of the plant are berry and which are not. This is a major consideration for a global industry that needs to produce enough coffee for a planet consuming an average of two billion cups per day. Its solution is dark-roasting: a sure-fire way to obliterate impurities (such as bugs, twigs, and leaves) on a large scale. Dark-roasting (sometimes to the point of blackness in very cheap coffees) also turns a naturally highly volatile product into something which looks and tastes "consistent" from batch to batch. The method has its pros and cons; while the industrial bean does have most of its nuance destroyed through this harsh process, it's also where what we think of as the "classic" bold, bitter, and nutty taste and flavor of coffee comes from. And while bitterness (a significant amount of which is down to the caffeine content itself) is to some extent a desirable attribute of all coffees, too much can be very unpleasant, not to mention often further exacerbated by poor brewing (particularly when it comes to espresso).

However, while the true complexity of coffee beans is far too unpredictable for the mainstream industry, which needs to offer consistency (one of the few characteristics coffee does not naturally boast), that same complexity is the source of a whole other world of coffee that embraces the full scope and depth of the bean. Higher standards of farming produce ripe, pure cherries (although these can only really be guaranteed by small-scale hand-picking), which makes lighter and more considered roasts possible. This kind of production preserves, accentuates, or controls the many unique characteristics and hundreds of aromatic compounds (more even than wine) of coffee. Identifying and describing these notes is an art in itself. A bean's natural acidity, for example, which may be sweet and round, or sharp like lemon, can be preserved through a light roast, or brought out as a desirable bitterness through a careful darker one. Its sweetness can be tart, like blueberries; its mouthfeel can be juicy, like tropical fruit; or its flavor profile malty, like a chocolate milkshake. Coffee beans are inherently extraordinarily complex, and great roasters know how to elevate the properties they want, and which combination of notes from different or single-origin beans will lend themselves to which brewing methods.

Beans selected for this kind of roasting—almost always Arabicas, although specialty Robustas do exist and are growing in popularity—are significantly more time-consuming and expensive to produce, and tend, therefore, to come mostly from smaller farms. These farms are often where the best practices tend to be found, so it's worth buying beans from independent producers wherever possible. This is not only ethical, in terms of the growers themselves and encouraging a better industry across the board, but also affects the quality and depth of what winds up in your cup.

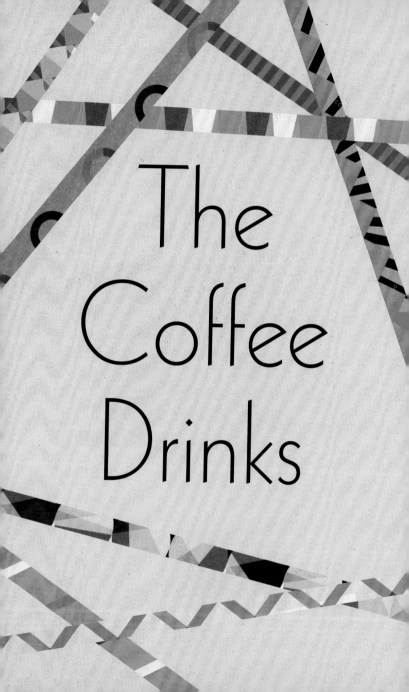

The
Coffee
Drinks

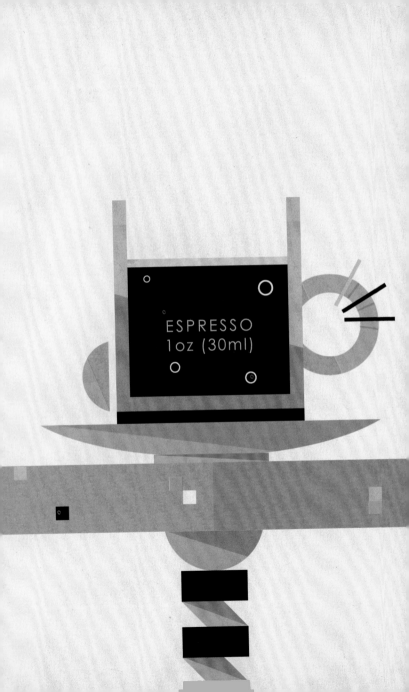

Espresso

The short, powerful espresso defines café culture, plays a significant part in national identities, and is the foundation of almost every coffee drink in cafés around the world. As well as being the workhorse of the coffee world, it's also widely thought to be the ultimate way to showcase the characteristics of quality coffee. Espresso is a deeply Italian invention, utilizing steam and enormous mechanized pressure to force water heated to the perfect temperature through coffee of exactly the right (very fine) grind consistency, all to produce something strong and inimitable. Good espresso is recognizable by its powerful aroma, a balance of desirable bitterness, body, and acidity, and its appearance (the surface should be topped with a luxurious golden emulsion of natural oils, known as *crema*). Whether served straight-up and standing at a coffee bar in Italy, as the base for a long Americano, or folded into frothy milk in a British greasy spoon, proper espresso can only come from intricate machinery, operated with care (and, in some cases, serious expertise).

Doppio

While in comparatively clumsy English we tend to ask for espresso in single or double form, the Italian words for these are *solo* and *doppio*.

A doppio is the same strength as a standard espresso, but twice as long—so 2oz (60ml). Two espresso shots will often be used in the base of a latte or cappuccino, and this quantity is in fact now so commonly used that it is widely thought to be the standard length for espresso. However, it's only when drunk straight-up that you'll tend to hear anybody use the correct name, and indeed, many places never do—so if asking for one ever leads to a blank face in response, just go for "double espresso."

Coffee Break

Coffee can be burned by the water with which it's brewed! This isn't much of a problem when using industrial, dark-roasted beans devoid of much or any complexity, but when they're on the lighter end of the scale, and therefore more nuanced, and bursting with characteristics, freshly boiled water should definitely be avoided to avoid ruining the flavor. The ideal brewing temperature is around 196–205°F (91–96°C), which is why you'll see baristas in specialty cafés using thermometers.

ESPRESSO
2oz (60ml)

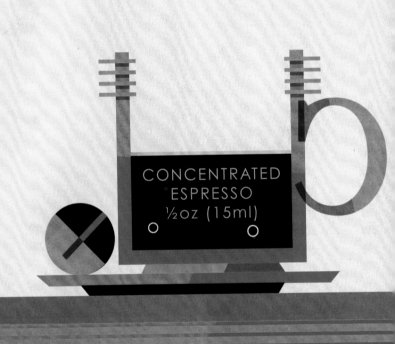

CONCENTRATED
ESPRESSO
½oz (15ml)

Ristretto

The Italian word *ristretto* may translate to "restricted," but the ristretto is absolutely not to be underestimated. It's made with the same amount of ground coffee as a solo shot of espresso, but only half the amount of water—making it only half the length, but the same strength. This different ratio and consequent pulling time (the process of water being forced through the coffee) means that the final product is more intense, but less bitter, than espresso, with noticeably different dominating characteristics due to fewer compounds being drawn from the coffee. Whether it's drunk straight-up or folded into microfoam (milk foamed with a steam wand on an espresso machine) to make a flat white, ristretto will have more body (roughly meaning the same as mouthfeel, which is, literally, how the coffee feels in your mouth), be less bitter, and offer a more rounded, naturally sweeter taste than espresso, making it perfect for milky drinks. It's both a distinctive and highly useful brewing method, and well worth noting for those exploring the coffee world.

Lungo

A lungo is effectively the inverse of ristretto: the same amount of ground coffee as espresso, but double the amount of water. The resulting coffee is noticeably less intense in taste, aroma, and appearance than espresso. However, because all the water included is brewed (meaning that none is added afterward), it does possess a fullness that a lengthened espresso-based drink, such as an Americano (espresso topped up with hot water) or long black (the inverse, to preserve the crema), won't. To go along with its length, lungo will take around double the pulling time of espresso—closer to a minute than the standard 20–30 seconds. Just as the ristretto's shorter pulling time makes it less bitter than espresso, the longer pulling time of the lungo (or *allongé*, as it's called in French after the phrase "to draw out") will often highlight the bitter characteristics of the beans.

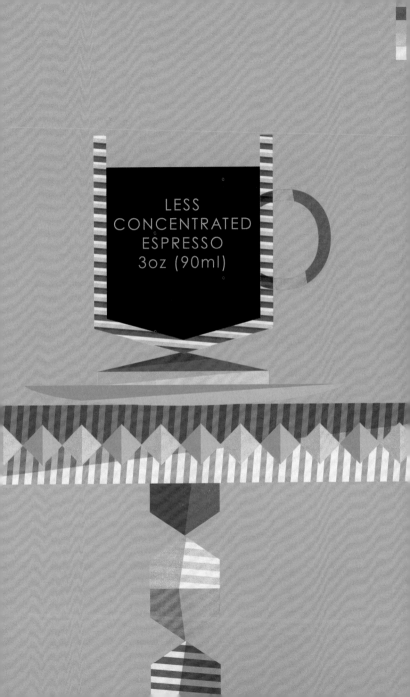

LESS
CONCENTRATED
ESPRESSO
3oz (90ml)

MILK
2½–3½oz
(75–100ml)

RISTRETTO
¾oz (20ml)

Piccolo

It might seem strange to think of a foodstuff as being cute, but there are few other words that so neatly fit the rarely found but memorable piccolo latte. There's unusual room for interpretation with the concept; all that's essential, really, is that it's a tiny, but consequently mighty, latte. Some baristas will make piccolo with single (or double) ristretto, for its short length and deep, rounded flavor, while others prefer a single espresso for its heightened and desirable bitterness. However, almost any piccolo-loving barista will tell you that what's most important is that the coffee base, whatever that may be, is topped up with the highest-quality whole milk to around 2½–3½oz (75–100ml)—less than half the standard 8oz (240ml) of a typical latte—and served in a demitasse glass. The piccolo is favored by those in the industry, such as head baristas or roasters, who need to taste coffee drinks continually throughout the day without overloading on rich milk. However, it's also adored by consumers (if they're lucky enough to come across it in the first place) who enjoy the distinct natural sweetness of whole milk with their coffee, but not to the extent that they want to drink full-on lattes every day.

Cortado

Cortado is arguably to many Latin nations what espresso is to the Italians. Cortado is most similar to piccolo, but with the key differences of being longer by around 1¾oz (50ml), more dense (the milk is not textured at all but simply steamed), based on espresso (as opposed to ristretto) for the full bite of the dark coffee usually used, and with cultural significance outside trendy coffee culture. Crucially, the cortado is designed to accentuate and elevate the espresso, in a similar way to the macchiato. Even the name— based on the Spanish verb *cortar,* meaning "to cut"—makes a point of the milk's job being functional: to temper the espresso's flavor and texture, not be the star of the show, as with the piccolo or flat white. While the cortado does very much now have a place on the blackboards of specialty coffee bars, its place in the world is one of accessibility; a short, simple milky coffee that's an essential part of daily life in many Spanish-speaking parts of the world, with plenty of variations such as the sweetened *cortadito* in Cuba (not to be confused with the unique Cuban espresso, which is often served with the same amount of milk but brewed with demerara sugar in the espresso pitcher).

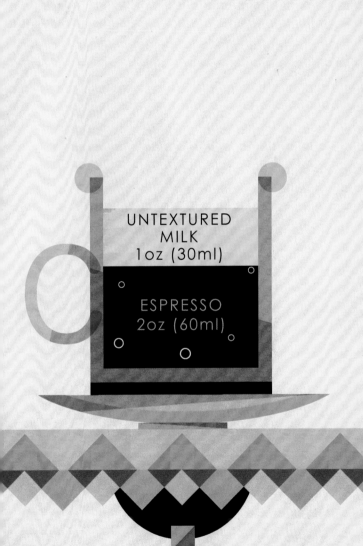

UNTEXTURED
MILK
1oz (30ml)

ESPRESSO
2oz (60ml)

MILK FOAM 1oz (30ml)

ESPRESSO
2oz (60ml)

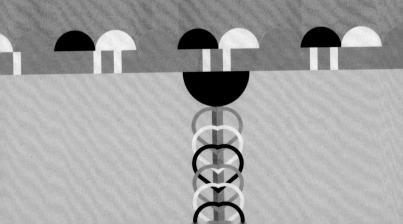

Macchiato

The intensity of espresso can be overwhelming on its own, particularly when it's pulled using beans with very distinctive notes of brightness or juiciness. Enter the macchiato, a subtle but effective recipe for mellowing the dazzling brightness (or sometimes overwhelming bitterness) of pure espresso. It achieves this using only a touch of slightly foamed milk (*caffè macchiato* in fact translates from Italian to "stained" or "spotted" coffee), which also adds a subtle, natural sweetness to the coffee without milk being the dominant element. A macchiato itself uses only one or two shots of espresso, and is barely longer than the lengths of the shots. In fact, the ratio of espresso to milk in a macchiato outstrips that of any other coffee drink made with milk. It's thought by many (especially in Italy) to be the best way to enjoy espresso, and is one of the most reliable ways to make very bitter beans more palatable, while keeping it as short as possible. Beyond the length, though, the concept of the coffee being "stained" by milk is key to what sets it apart from the piccolo or cortado—in a macchiato, the espresso remains the star, with the milk being there simply to uplift it.

Americano

At some point in the 21st century, the word *Americano* became synonymous with black coffee—which is not, in fact, accurate. Americano is simply the espresso-based answer to brewed coffee. Through the ever-growing advent of the espresso machine, Americano has become one of the most common forms of long coffee on main (high) streets, in restaurants, and indeed at home. The given (but unproven) story behind the name—which, you'll have correctly guessed, loosely means "American" coffee— is that American soldiers stationed in Italy during World War II would water down the local espresso to match the strength of the brewed coffee to which they were accustomed at home. However, although the strengths and caffeine contents are roughly the same, the flavor of Americano differs from standard brewed coffee; Americano will have more body, and usually a richer taste, but also likely come with more bitterness from the harsher extraction. Some espresso or ristretto suits Americano brilliantly; some badly, in much the same way that some beans will make a better brew than others. Whatever happens, it's not about the drink's color—an Americano with milk added is still very much an Americano.

HOT WATER
3oz (90ml)

ESPRESSO
2oz (60ml)

BREWED COFFEE
4oz (120ml)

ESPRESSO
2oz (60ml)

Red Eye

Without being too dramatic, red-eye coffee is a little like being in love: if it's something you've ever experienced, you'll know, and not forget about it in a hurry. It refers to the somewhat unholy union of a single espresso and brewed coffee—yes, lengthening an already strong shot with yet more caffeine (instead of simply hot water, as with Americano). The resulting drink can, believe it or not, have quite an effect on the brain, hence the appropriate name "red-eye" (a term usually referring to long overnight flights which leave the passengers feeling particularly wired). And that's not even the end of the story; adding a second espresso shot will turn a red-eye into a black-eye and a third (seriously, be careful here) into a dead-eye.

Coffee Break

Plenty of cities around the world identify with their coffee culture, but a 2012 study by the team behind Eatery, a food-tracking app, showed that New Yorkers are probably the most justified in this—drinking almost seven times more coffee than any other city in the world.

Café Breve

The café breve (pronounced brev-ay) or breve latte is an American twist on a standard latte. Somewhat endearingly, this twist is based on incorporating rich cream into the already milky mix. It's common in the US for a mixture known as half-and-half to be used, which—being literally a 50:50 mix of milk and cream—can be made at home as well as bought from stores. The idea may make some recoil in horror at the thought of its calorie content, but the café breve is more than just indulgence for the sake of indulgence; half-and-half is dense, rich, and naturally sweet, making the resulting coffee a distinctive luxury quite unlike any other in the coffee world.

Coffee Break

Coffee has been present in one way or another for many of history's great moments, but one in particular wins: the birth of the webcam. The webcam was set up by students at the University of Cambridge, not to contact distant family members, but to check whether their communal coffee pot was full, saving them a trip if they were feeling too lazy to be the one to make a fresh pot. Students.

HALF-AND-HALF
6oz (180ml)

ESPRESSO
6oz (180ml)

MILK FOAM 2oz (60ml)

STEAMED MILK
2oz (60ml)

ESPRESSO
2oz (60ml)

Cappuccino

The light, frothy, ubiquitous cappuccino is perhaps the grandfather of modern café culture; once thought of as the height of sophistication, and now something thought of (fondly) as being slightly old-fashioned. It's also got about the longest history of any distinct coffee drink, dating back to at least 18th-century Vienna, long before the invention of the espresso machine with which the modern cappuccino is made. These early versions were made with strong brewed coffee, whipped cream, and various spices. Its original Viennese name, *kapuziner* (an obvious foreshadowing of its modern form), referred to the mixed drink's distinctive brown color, which was similar to the robes worn by Capuchin monks. The cappuccino as we know it—made with double espresso and steamed milk, topped up with a significant quantity of milk foam, and sometimes dusted with chocolate powder—made waves throughout Europe and America over the course of the 20th century, and although it has now rather had its day in terms of sophistication, it's still a vital part of the coffee family, as most grandfathers are.

Caffè Latte

No matter what sort of coffee shop one enters—
swanky or grimy, specialty or cheap—it's
effectively a given that you'll find two styles on
the menu: cappuccino and (under one name
or another) latte. Both are as common and
important to café culture as each other, and
while the former includes a significant amount
of foamed milk, latte tends to be made up of a
smoother combination of almost entirely espresso
and steamed milk, with little to no foam. Coffee
and milk have long been used together across
European cultures, under various names and in
various deceptively similar forms, some of which
will be explained over the coming pages. The
latte, however, almost always means one thing:
a long, espresso-based milky coffee, with enough
on top to allow a practiced barista to leave
intricate works of art on the surface. The name
is a short version of the Italian name "caffè latte"
—a distinction which, in its homeland, is essential,
for asking simply for latte in Italy will get you a
glass of milk (even, in some more old-school
places, when they know what you mean).

MILK FOAM
(optional)

STEAMED MILK
3–6oz
(90–180ml)

ESPRESSO
2oz (60ml)

STEAMED MILK
5oz (150ml)

FRESH COFFEE
5oz (150ml)

Café au Lait

To the untrained eye, the concept of *café au lait* (French for, literally, "coffee with milk") may seem identical to the Italian latte. However, café au lait, with its genuine myriad names across Europe (*milchkaffee* in Germany or *café con leche* in Spain, is arguably more ubiquitous than either latte or cappuccino, and about as flexible a form of milk and coffee as is possible—referring usually to brewed coffee with hot milk added. However, café au lait's flexibility across the coffee world means that variations exist all over the globe, and in many places it has been made with espresso since the machine's advent—but with a less distinct style or appearance than latte (most notably with no art on top). Café au lait is a functional, accessible, wholly unpretentious drink, and possibly the broadest, most open-to-interpretation form of coffee with milk; in certain parts of the US, it's even brewed with endive (chicory), or served in a bowl to emphasize its European-ness.

MICROFOAM
5oz (150ml)

DOUBLE RISTRETTO
1oz (30ml)

Flat White

The flat white has graduated from being a mysterious, intriguing newcomer to the coffee world, and settled into place as the elegant star of most café menus. It's made up of a powerful (usually double) ristretto shot and moderately lengthened milk, which is steamed into a microfoam (this is far smoother and more velvety than the froth of a cappuccino) and folded through the coffee—but the milk used cannot be just any milk. It must contain enough fat and protein to create the incomparably rich body which defines a flat white, and therefore be of the best quality available. The texture of a flat white is silky, light, and one of the most refined ways to bring out and experience the characteristics of good espresso. It's a challenge to perfect, but this practice is worth a barista's time, given that the flat white is widely thought to be the pinnacle of milky coffee.

Mocha

Coffee and sweetness are, for many, a match made in heaven, so it stands to reason that a drink of coffee mixed with chocolate would exist. Mocha (or mochaccino) gets a bad name in the specialty coffee scene, but when made with the right coffee and quality ingredients, it can be a delight. It is usually espresso-based, with chocolate (or the flavor of chocolate) incorporated at some point in the process. This can come from mixing chocolate powder into the espresso base and topping the whole thing up with whole milk, or, when things are done properly, by replacing a certain amount of steamed milk in a latte-style coffee with real melted chocolate. However, the mocha is one of those coffee drinks open to experimentation and interpretation, and can be made with or include bittersweet (dark) chocolate, white chocolate, or a mix of the two (sometimes known as a marble or zebra mocha). It is also often served with either a simple, cappuccino-style, foamed-milk top, or a decoration bordering on the garish; think whipped cream, shaved chocolate, chocolate sauce, and marshmallows.

1–2 TEASPOONS
CHOCOLATE POWDER
OR SYRUP

STEAMED MILK
5oz (150ml)

ESPRESSO
2oz (60ml)

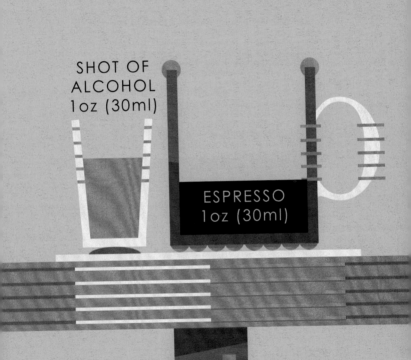

SHOT OF
ALCOHOL
1oz (30ml)

ESPRESSO
1oz (30ml)

Caffè Corretto

Coffee with booze tends to unite coffee lovers across the world. Some, as we'll see, are almost dangerously indulgent, but the Italian version —just like the espresso itself—is short, efficient, and straightforward: coffee, straight liquor, and usually nothing else. Caffè corretto usually appears as a 50:50 partnering of espresso and grappa, although brandy and sambuca are also often used. The two will usually be served side by side in a small cup and shot glass respectively, as opposed to being mixed by the server, although this is not always the case. The fact that the name *corretto* sounds similar to the English word "correct" is no accident; *caffè corretto*, amusingly, means "corrected coffee"—yes, as in "coffee made correct by the addition of booze."

Irish Coffee

There's no debate over how the Irish coffee—
an impossibly comforting, sinful blend of strong
brewed coffee, Irish whiskey, sugar, and thick
cream—came into the world in 1943. When
a flight out of Shannon Airport was canceled
during a harsh winter night, a local chef named
Joe Sheridan began adding whiskey to the
hot coffee he was serving to the stranded
passengers, and named it "Irish" on the spot
when asked by one comforted drinker if it was a
Brazilian style of coffee. Soon after, it was picked
up by an American travel writer passing through
Shannon Airport, and the rest is coffee history.
What makes drinking (proper) Irish coffee special
is that the hot, boozy coffee is drawn through
the thick, ice-cold cream, which must be poured
over the back of a spoon, so as to spread evenly
over and rest on the surface.

1 TABLESPOON
BROWN SUGAR

CREAM 2oz (60ml)

IRISH WHISKEY
2oz (60ml)

BLACK COFFEE
5oz (150ml)

TOP UP WITH
WHIPPED CREAM

ESPRESSO
2oz (60ml)

Vienna Coffee

One of the most prominent sites in the history of coffee is Vienna, Austria, where café culture is listed by a branch of UNESCO as something of "Intangible Cultural Heritage." The coffee drink eponymous with the city is appropriately indulgent: two shots of dark espresso, topped up to brimming point with cold whipped cream, and usually (in a style fairly fitting for the lavish décor of Vienna and its coffeehouses) decorated with chocolate sprinkles. The drinking experience is not unlike that of an Irish coffee, but due to the strength and length gained by using espresso rather than brewed coffee, it's shorter, sharper, and more impactful.

Coffee Break

Coffee is a fuel for the masses, but it's also gone hand-in-hand with intellectualism for a long time. J. S. Bach wrote a short opera by way of an ode to the drink (at a time when Viennese coffeehouses were seen as a scourge of decent society); Benjamin Franklin loved spending leisure time conversing, holding meetings, and writing in coffeehouses in 18th-century London; and French philosopher Voltaire famously claimed to drink around 50 cups a day (probably avoid trying that one yourself).

Affogato

Affogato—an individual Italian dessert made by pouring espresso over vanilla ice-cream—falls into that impertinent category of recipes which always blow diners away, but are as straightforward to prepare as they look. In fact, there's really only one rule to achieving a great affogato: good, bold espresso and better ice-cream. The magic of the dessert (although there are ongoing disagreements in Italy over whether it is a dessert or, in fact, a drink) is that the familiar, luxurious richness of slowly melting ice-cream is accelerated by the heat of the coffee, which brings with it the familiar bold, bitter flavor of espresso; a combination upon which a whole world of milky coffee drinks is based. Naturally, affogato can include a dash or full shot of booze —usually amaretto—which, just as fans of the Irish coffee know, is a winning combination. The affogato has an indispensable performance element, too, through the spectacle of "drowning" (the translation of the Italian name) the ice-cream at the table, with the espresso's dark body and rich golden crema marbling into the melting ice-cream.

1 SCOOP
VANILLA
ICE-CREAM

ESPRESSO
2oz (60ml)

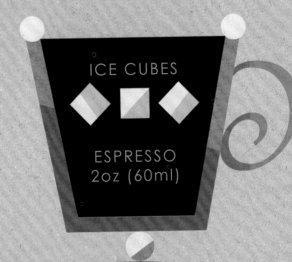

ICE CUBES

ESPRESSO
2oz (60ml)

Café con Hielo

There are almost countless ways to make and serve cold coffee, but the Spanish one, "coffee with ice," is one of the more distinctive due to its inclusion of ice cubes or chips. Like most iced-coffee styles, it is espresso-based—mostly because the melting ice immediately begins to lessen the intensity of the coffee, and unless brewed doubly strong, it will be bland, bitter, and unpleasant. Café con hielo tends to be served as a straight-up double espresso, and is (usually heavily) sweetened by the drinker while the espresso is still hot. A glassful of ice on the side will then be (carefully) covered with the hot mixture and stirred, also by the drinker. If milk is desired, this will need to be specifically requested, and will also be served on the side, to be added last. It's a pleasant, personal ritual, preparing your own café con hielo, and one that only the most practiced drinkers can perform without making a spot of mess on the countertop.

Cold Brew

If there's an opposite to the high-pressure, rapid extraction of espresso, it's cold-brewing. In fact, while most brewing methods focus on quickly extracting as much from the beans as possible by introducing them to hot water and drinking the result there and then, cold-brewing really is cold from start to finish. This slows down and tempers the infusion enormously, producing an incomparably subtle, nuanced drink that's naturally sweeter and significantly less bitter than any other coffee. The lower levels of acidity and bitterness afforded by this cold infusion also mean the product can be stored in the fridge, and still be delicious a week later. Making your own is simple, but takes patience; the grounds must be steeped in fresh, cold water, at a roughly 1:8 ratio, for a minimum of 18 hours, and ideally a full 24. Cold-brewing calls for an inordinately coarse grind to avoid sediment, and even then requires thorough straining (ideally several times through a clean muslin or cheesecloth) to ensure the final product is clear, sweet, and satisfying in the way that only cold brew can be. Whether it's served straight-up or marbled with cold milk over ice, or even carefully heated after brewing and served hot, cold brew is an inimitable form of brewed coffee that's well worth the wait.

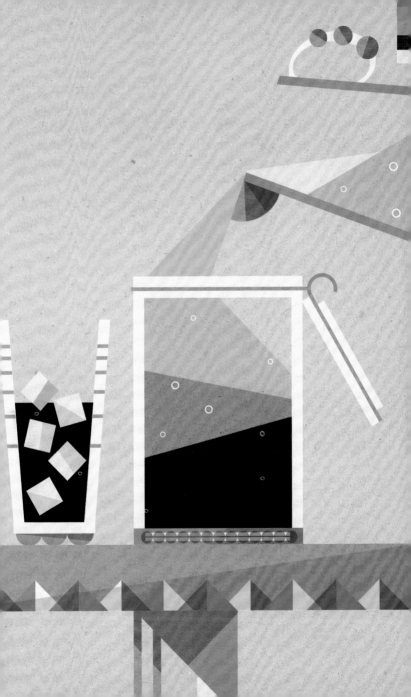

Stovetop

Brewing apparatuses are all fairly distinctive, but there's possibly nothing more quintessentially European in coffee than the stovetop, or moka pot. Made usually from aluminum or stainless steel, the main strength of the stovetop brewer lies in its compactness (its Italian name, *macchinetta*, literally translates as "small machine"). It uses steam pressure and a cleverly designed valve system to heat cold water and force it upward through a compact bed of coffee, producing an espresso-length drink at home without the need for expensive machinery. However, it's important to distinguish between a stovetop-brew and true espresso, for while the pressure of the former can produce a little crema, it is nowhere near intense or rapid enough to produce what constitutes espresso. It does have similarities, however, namely in that what is produced will be quite strong, and calls for a very fine grind. While moka pots are incredibly durable, and can last for a lifetime (or, as many families will tell you, even longer), it is crucial that they are cleaned thoroughly and regularly to avoid oil build-up, which will spoil the taste of the coffee and eventually the entire machine itself.

French Press

The French press, or cafetière is, despite its name, another classic Italian design like the moka pot, made up of a (usually glass) pot and a relatively coarse strainer (sieve) attached to a plunger. The design may have its origins in the late 1920s, but the basic elements of the brewing method —allowing coarse grounds to be steeped in and then filtered from hot water using a strainer—is one of the oldest ways of producing coffee, and far less complex a system than that of the moka pot or espresso machine. While variables (such as preheating the flask with boiling water, or an incorrect grind consistency) will affect the outcome, the margin for error with a French press is about as wide as it gets. As with stovetop brewers, however, it is essential that a French press—particularly its filter—is kept meticulously clean to avoid a nasty, over-bitter coffee.

Coffee Break

The fact that coffee beans are the seeds of the *Coffea* berry means they're technically—*technically*—a fruit. This is really true in the same way that wine being made from grapes makes it a fruit, so unfortunately it's probably best to be careful before substituting the fruit in your diet for either.

AeroPress

Everyone knows the story of the ugly duckling.
Well, the AeroPress is the coffee world's very
own, widely beloved, and reasonably new-on-
the-scene ugly duckling, with a cylindrical body
made from functional plastic that is both near-
indestructible and easy to clean. It balances
quality and efficiency arguably better than
any other brewer. Its method is actually most
similar in principle to that of the French press, but
takes a leaf from both espresso and pour-over
technology by creating a vacuum which forces
briefly steeped coffee through a purpose-made
filter. Like the French press, this method calls for
a coarse grind to avoid sediment, but when
the standard paper filter is used (as opposed to
reusable metal ones), next to none of this can
make it through anyway. Both filter types also
catch infinitely more of the coffee's natural oils
than the strainer (sieve) of the French press,
making for a far clearer cup and, as is widely
agreed, an extraordinary cup of brewed coffee.

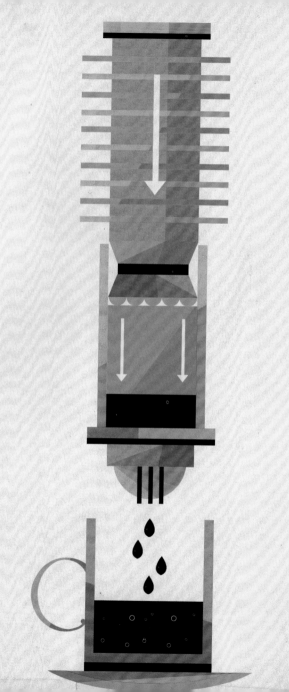

Pour-over

Pour-over is another form of brewed coffee, wherein (as the name suggests) hot water is poured slowly over coarse grounds and allowed to drip down through a paper filter into some kind of receptacle. This combination of a very gentle brewing method and a very fine filter produces an exquisitely pure, clean coffee, and for this reason, pour-over is a style of brewed coffee adored by the specialty industry. In such circles, pour-over appears either in the form of a V60 cone—which sits directly over the cup and features ridges down the inside to give the coffee and water the perfect amount of contact time—or the striking Chemex brewing flask, which is still thought of as a triumph of modern design, and has a permanent spot at the Museum of Modern Art in New York City. However, while pour-over brewing can be fairly showy and specialist, it is actually closer than many may think to the large, efficient coffee machines used in diners and homes across America and parts of Europe, which use a very similar method to produce big pots that sit on a hot-plate for hours (although this is referred to as "drip coffee," rather than pour-over).

Siphon Brewing

Despite having been invented in the 1830, the siphon or vacuum coffee-maker still looks like a brewing device from the future. Its various elements have had many interpretations and guises, but the core method remains the same: it always utilizes two glass chambers, vapor pressure, and a vacuum to produce incredible coffee. The siphon splits opinion, being seen by many as an extraordinary feat of engineering, and by others as absurdly complicated and cumbersome. Indeed, due to their complexity, siphons are now very rarely used, despite once being reasonably popular in 20th-century cafés (although even devotees will admit it was never for their practicality or efficiency). However, whether the filter used by a particular siphon is the beautiful, glass-rod style, or one made from cloth, metal mesh, or paper, they produce an exceptionally clear coffee, and the process alone is a mesmerizing spectacle. In fact, whenever siphons are used, they tend to take pride of place on the countertop—and really, given the many methods of brewing coffee which prioritize efficiency, what's wrong with showing off a little?

Index